COUNTRY OF MEMORY

COUNTRY OF MEMORY

CHARLES FISHMAN

Seattle, WA

Copyright 2004 by Charles Fishman

Published by Uccelli Press
P.O. Box 85394
Seattle, WA 98145-1394
866-206-2311 (toll free)
206-240-0075 (voice)
206-361-5001 (fax)
pub@uccellipress.com
www.uccellipress.com

All rights reserved. Except for brief passages quoted in a newspaper, magazine, radio, or television review, no part of this book may be reproduced in any form or by any means, electronic or mechanical, including photocopying and recording, or by any information storage and retrieval system, without permission in writing from the publisher.

Published in the United States of America

ISBN 0-9723231-3-9
Library of Congress Control Number: 2004102421

First Uccelli Press Printing, 2004
Printed by Central Plains Book Mfg, Winfield, KS

Cover image : *Invisible Cities I (Man on Bicycle),* 1993,
Oil on wood, 14 1/4" x 20 1/4"
by Thomas Germano
Cover photograph by Vincent P. Ombres
Book design and editing by Toni La Ree Bennett

For my parents,
who must still be dancing . . .

ACKNOWLEDGMENTS

Grateful acknowledgment is made to the editors of the following periodicals, in which some of the poems in this book first appeared: *Asheville Poetry Review, Big City Lit, College English, The Drunken Boat, Full Circle, International Quarterly, Jerseyworks, Kota Press Poetry Journal, Liberty Hill Poetry Review, Midstream, Milkweed Review, Natural Bridge, New Works Review, On the Page (PSA), The Pedestal Magazine, Petroglyph, Poetry Now, Poetry Porch, Raccoon, Rattapallax, Recursive Angel, Red River Review, Samsara Quarterly, Sidereality, TheScreamOnline, Southern Poetry Review, Three Candles, Valparaiso Poetry Review, Verse.*

"Blue Bicycles" and "Moose-Moon, Montana" first appeared in *Zoom* (Singular Speech Press, 1990).

My gratitude to the Jack Kerouac Writer-in-Residence Foundation, the Millay Colony for the Creative Arts, the Ucross Foundation, and the Virginia Center for the Creative Arts, for time, space, and support that allowed some of the poems in this collection to be written.

TABLE OF CONTENTS

1. Through the Ice

2. After Darkness

3. At the Edge

4. In Unknown Tongues

. . . all substance thins into mist
and has its vague frontiers,
the country of memory.
—Derek Walcott

Beginning with a Line by Eugenio Montejo

In the lost land of my absent family,
I hear a bell ringing. It's a bell ringing
in the dark morning of a world long gone
a bird singing from a branch that swings
and creaks in a forgotten century
it's birdsong that chimes like a near
or distant bell   and it's a voice that speaks
from the lost land of being and memory
where a vanished family lives   it's a word
composed of two syllables that breathe
in the soft light of this gray morning
on which I am born: *Dearson,* it sings,
bell-like in resonance and clarity, *Dearson,*
it rings like a bird on a branch in the wind,
and I cannot speak to this voice   to this bell
swinging in the light of the vanquished past
to this birdsong that fills me with joy
and sorrow.

1. Through the Ice

CHARLES FISHMAN

In the Woods, 1951

I remember how the light pawed down
through densely tangled branches
and how the narrow creek jangled
over its scatter of burnished stones
worn to a smoothness in the cold churn
of water. The day began when school ended

and our feet sank into fern banks
and leaf-mulch or squelched in bog-holes
of aromatic muck. We leapt over moss-
crushed oaks   white-barked paper birches
climbed wind-sheared hickories and beeches

and, in the green drench of summer,
swam naked in our garden. In that clear water
that granted every pardon, we gashed our hearts
and came up gasping, the afternoon sun

encircling our foreheads with tendrils of molten gold.
We heard drums in the leaf-tops that spoke of endings,
yet we lived as if time was not our master, as if

we were kings of the forest   and not its slowly drowning sons.

Learning to Swim

Zach's Bay, 1951

Field 5 – Jones Beach: it was there,
amid the thousands, I found the power
to survive.

I remember tip-toeing on the edge
blanket to blanket   on burning sand
under a blazing sun

then wading in hip-deep water
that nearly steamed   In July's torrid heat
I left the earth behind

and pushed toward the vague horizon
until the faint hiss of waves slapping
an old barrier fence

forced me to wake   It all comes back—
how I fought the water, smacking it with my fists,
as if the inlet had a face

battering it   smashing water into water
yelling to be saved   It comes back: how no one
came to the rescue

how I kept my head above the turbid surface
and splashed shorewards   abandoned
but alive.

CHARLES FISHMAN

At the Levittown Pool, 1952

This is where I first fell in love
with people—with their idiosyncrasies
of size and shape   their queer off-
balance walks   their high-pitched
and raucous laughs   and it was here
I fell in love with flesh: how it pushed
and sagged and bulged against nylon
and tried to escape

This was the place I became
most human: leaping with friends
into the piss-laced water we splashed
into waves   racing   in a chlorine
haze   from one end of the pool
to the other   standing on our hands
in an all-male underwater ballet

The lifeguard's screeching whistle
would echo in our heads   and the molten
August sun   would send down its fire
The glory was to be young   and dazed
with life   which swam unbroken circles
around us   and would not let us drown.

Through the Ice, 1953

In memory of Skipper Broich

I think of you now: how your short life ended,
as if on schedule. While you lived,
something invisible seemed to batter you—

a demon or force field that smashed you
against every wall. Yet it's not the car
crashes or concussions I recall

but a scene, like a circle of ice, sawn
from the frozen past, its edges jagged, its hues,
even then, minimal, now bleached to a dwindling fire

of colors . . . Do you remember
how you almost died late on that winter evening?
how the thin crust of blacker ice broke under you

and you dropped in the dark so deep on your downward journey?
We'd been coasting all day on some white-dark hill
between trees that brushed our faces

and were walking quickly toward the shortcut
through the woods that lay on the bank of the lake
we trekked over like travelers in the Arctic.

In our triple-knotted boots, our wool scarves
and scuffed bomber jackets, we trudged toward home,
toward the dim light over familiar doorways

and the rich aromas of food our mothers cooked
at the first tinge of twilight. The January sun sank
in slow gradations, each slight hint of darkening a tick

on the clock of childhood. Skipper, you must have been
more hungry, more tired, or just plain younger,
and ran ahead of us to where the thin fabric of ice

ripped into sheer strips of translucent frost.
Shocked to stillness, we held back, then rushed
to where you'd vanished   and then returned.

It must have been your brother who calmed you,
who begged you to settle deeper into coldness,
to trust his high and broken voice. Yes,

it must have been Dave who promised
we'd rescue you, who slid his Red Ranger sled
into that gaping hole in the universe

where it found your hands.

The Pearl Harbor Kid

Aldo Rossi, 1953

On that day I snapped his photo,
he could recall the way—12 years earlier—
lamps in the delivery room at the base hospital
quivered, like bells being rung, how they
swung in the un-breeze rushing in

from the Pacific, and how they sent out
blue tides of sparks. The shock of his arrival
left no physical scar, but you had to watch out
for that wryly challenging smile, that cockiness
no joke or jibe could deflate, the light in those dark

Italian eyes. See, here he is again on our nearly
vacant street, striking that trademark pose,
the Babe Ruth bat held smartly on his shoulder.
Clearly, it is late winter, maybe March, for the few
recently planted trees remain leafless.

Yet baseball was surely on Aldo's mind that day:
a kind of pre-spring fever that couldn't be cured
without playing. Look at the cloth coat he wears,
its mock-fur collar limp and faded, the way
every crease and seam flexes under the pull

of that just-frozen swing. He's wearing good
brown shoes that are going to get murdered
on macadam. Notice how neatly the laces
are tied, how securely he stands and waits:
he has all day for the ball to reach him.

Perhaps Aldo has just come home from church
or a visit to his grandmother—yes, maybe that's it:
this must be a late March Sunday, not yet time
for supper: he wears his best pair of jeans,
the bottoms 'rolled' in a six-inch fold that exposes

the washed-blue underhue of denim. Leaning forward
in the batter's box of the 50s, Aldo seems to tower
over the houses, over the luckless lawns, over
the compass-true sidewalks . . . yet who is this boy
but a phantom out of childhood, a tossed ball

on opening day somehow stilled in flight?

A Family Outing

Long Island, early 1950s

A summer day   and Mom gets lost
on the parkway   It's getting late:
the time when shadows gather   One
more turn, and we're at Pilgrim State
In the back seat, Harriet and I grin
at each other: *Is she making a delivery?*
Maybe Aunt Edna, who sits up front,
on edge as usual   with all her grievances
showing   When you're eleven or eight,
you don't know it can be you   Darkness
creeps in a little under the arched
entranceway to the hospital   where the car
is parked   but running   Now Edna is
cracking up   the tears are streaming
and Mom, good sport that she is, is
already in stitches: their laughter a cross
between howling and weeping   Whatever
this disease is, it must be catching: Harriet's
snorting and shrieking   Edna's choking
and hacking   Mom's slapping the wheel
with both red hands   and I can barely breathe
in the face of this hysteria   It's a great time
to be alive   when the signs shift and a new
reality encroaches: who can find her way home
then? When Mom gets us rolling again, we
fall silent: ready to be admitted at last
to this house of dementia and heartbreak.

This House

Potted plants dot the living room window
and at the corner of the house a few roses

have bloomed, but outside my parents' home
the white flowerbox remains empty   and inside

nothing is blossoming   Out of the bedrock
of the 50s, our house rises: eight years have passed

since the terror of war began to recede   and my sister
was born   I know she is curled up and asleep

under her bright quilt in the back room
where two curtained windows open on the ghosts

of morning   It must be April or May 1953:
spring grass rubs green darkness into the day

and the glare pouring in from the west—the glare
that blurs all edges—is the sign of deliverance

or forgetfulness   Over a slow cigarette, Mother
dreams in the kitchen: the mail will not arrive for hours

nor will Father return from the daily siege of his life
before night sifts down   and grass deepens its hold

on the season   In this house, as always, it is the past.

A Photo of Isidore, 1953

After so many years, why do you linger?

I remember you wearing flannel shirts
and loose wool slacks   and puttering
in your Colgate Avenue apartment
yet, Grandfather, here you are
on this concrete walk   posed
with your head in the sky

Here you are   in your double-breasted suit
appearing formal and remote   but strong
and solid, too   not any kind of ghost
So much life   still beats in you

But I know this year will be your last
that your white hair   and wire-rimmed
glasses   are fading   and your callused hands
are losing their grasp: despite your starched
collar and tied cravat, death is coming
I remember how you left me   with so many
unanswered questions

And, Grandfather, I'm uncertain still:
What were your parents' names   the *shtetl*
where you lived   the dreams that sailed
with you? I know nothing about your life
about your trials growing up   about Anna,
your first wife: what promises did you break,
and did she wait for you?

You stand on the front walk   of an almost forgotten
house   a leaf that will not open   Reach out
to me now   through the torn veil of language.

Words

In your closed mouth, father,
I found words: long words
that described small islands
short words that embraced
the deepest desires   esoteric
words   that transported me
to microambient worlds   words
that worshipped   and despaired
that were toxins ointments salves
words stripped from rare
ecclesiastical bindings   or ripped
from the air.

I loved words as much as you
loved silence: words that wakened
intoxicated   explored   words
with the rank smell of viscera
that excoriated   and restored
I collected words, forged from gold
or zirconium   words ethereal as breath
and dark plutonium words   more fatal
than death   Words my daggers
my lariats   my fire-scorched tongs
my antlers   my cockscomb   my
rhinoceros horn   words my plunging beak
my wild and thorny cry.

My Father on a Sled, Smoking

Winter 1953

There he is on the sled, which is parked
on the front lawn. He's going nowhere fast,
yet the reins are in his hands—no, not
the reins but the rope this small vehicle
is towed with. And he's a happy man—
anyone who motors by can see that:
the way he sits erect, his knees jutting
but not quite skyward, his feet in rubber
boots, jammed to the rudder and ready
to steer. The weather is mild and clear.

Now look at the lit cigarette that droops
from his lips that resist speaking, at his
ungloved hands that revel in their strength
and will not heed the cold. My father
is not yet old though, unknown to him,
he is dying: if he continues to smoke
like this, his lungs will wither and blacken
his hands fall open in his lap. Though the day
is frozen in memory, his world is rushing
forward. Father, this is no time to relax.
Stand up now: you need to wrest control

from this poisoned future. Pitch the fresh pack
hidden in your jacket into the glitter of ice
and snow. Take off your cap and let it go.
Breathe in the sweet chill of this undreamt of
moment when life offers you a choice. Father,
listen to my voice that calls out to you
across the snow-bound void: you will swerve
at the last jolting second, and death's branches
will scar your face but, five decades later,
you will sit, knees wrapped in a white wool blanket:
a dear scared frail old man, dozing to Frank Sinatra
and almost at peace as sleep drags you down.

All American

He was a good-looking man,
and he was easy to be with:
on a hike, on a bike trail,
on a deep-sea journey
into black fathoms.

When he smiled, he smiled
from the bottom of his life
where northwest rivers flashed
in the rain of childhood.
He grew up clean, clear-headed,

strong in the presence of brothers,
and did not carry with him a sack
of shattered dreams or broken vessels
that could no longer hold sparks
or parchments of some dark tribal history.

The sun, when it was shining, pooled
at his feet, and he could wisecrack
with the best of them: the good ol' boys
he'd meet in the Air Force radio shack
in Clear, Alaska (so cold in that place

that piss would freeze) or the aircraft
warriors at Boeing Everett, in the Lower
48, who pledged their sacred honor—
and their overtime—to the nation's need
for flight, to fire-power without limit,

and to the bottom line. He was a born-
again believer in Bible real estate
and a picture postcard patriot
of the American Way. Sister, this is
the man who would father your children

and stand at your side in the changeable
weather of decades, who would grieve
with you gone. For him, *love*
was an active verb, *family* and *country*—
indivisible nouns.

Saturday Matinee, 1954

Each week, I trekked from Forest City
to *The Meadowbrook*: up Oakfield Avenue

past Lily Canale's place next to the radio tower:
past the gas station at the corner of North Jerusalem

and, further north, the deli, cleaner's, shoe repair, luncheonette
hunched at a bend in the road: past the Carvel's

that seemed to have fallen from the sky onto Hempstead Turnpike
and the red-and-white ice cream parlor that floated on the planet

like an ark—I rushed past them all to where a small temple
rose out of glass and concrete.

Such hymns to cowboy courage were sung in there! Such psalms
to love and war! In that almost virgin country I saw each Saturday,

a horse thief could be elected judge—even president—
and the massacre of Comanches by our cavalry was reason enough

to crow. In that 50s version of suburban childhood, sex
was still distant and mysterious—a trickling brook that babbled

in a hidden grove—but then the house lights dimmed,
the staticky speakers warmed, a popcorn incense wafted

from the balcony, and the holy screen was unveiled. Darkness
would enter then and do battle, and the theater would lift a little

in that turbulence. There was no priest but the projectionist,
his one good sermon delivered, *sotto voce,*

in pale blue smoke that pulsed like rays from a star.

Learning to Dance, 1956

It was the 50s, and all of us
were kids, but you were older—
almost a woman—and you would

teach me to dance. You were
the dark-haired child in a family
of blondes, slightly exotic, wilder,

my best friend's sister.
In your father's basement,
you took my hand and showed me

how to hold you—how to hold
a woman. I was fourteen and knew
already how to be awkward. You knew

I was falling into shadows. When I breathed
your hair, I was no longer in the forest
but had broken through

to a clearing where tall grasses whispered
and swayed, where white-petalled daisies
and violet clover blossomed.

You moved me deeper into the music
and made a meadow spring up around me.
Your body showed me that I had strength

to change the moment, if only the quiet
power of a summer breeze . . .
When you said I would be a good dancer,

that I had *rhythm* that I could *swing,*
I held you close: some day,
I would find the one

who would pull me near to her in love,
not mercy; I would dance with her
and learn her secret names.

Breaking Windows, 1957

I remember when Dave and I discovered
the splintered wrecks of oaks, the broken shafts
of beeches—trees we had climbed and, by the rights
of boyhood, claimed: how the pain of that moment
thumped against our hearts with the heft of arrowheads.

Through closed eyes, we saw leaves in their green shadows,
the sway of branches under a deep blue sky, dappled sunlight
and rich black earth that had held us in every season:
all of it lost, without a word from us. And so, Dave, Paul,
Skipper, and I, on bikes without reflectors,

in early darkness—the opaque dark of a hidden moon—
took rocks that steel blades had scooped from this place
no longer ours, and smashed each pane in the new school's
face. We threw each rock with a childish fury
that would outlast boyhood, the 60s, marriage,

and divorce. We threw with a cold force that only
our own children's questioning gazes could stop.

Paul Granger's Wound

You were the smallest, Paul—
the shortest, leanest, blondest, bravest
in our crew—and you have retreated less far
into darkness. I remember the day
that would etch your wound into my mind,
each catch and notch of memory glistening
with your blood. There was bright sunlight
and deep blue sky   a blaze of white roses
and the dark gray haze of the new state road
the highway commission had bulldozed
into our lives.

You were wearing a round-necked polo shirt
and rolled-up jeans, a black leather belt
and high-backed sneakers. Zigzag stripes crested
on your chest in vertical waves that flowed
from neck to groin: a map of some watery terrain
no friend or parent could decipher. I remember
how the dark blue denim rippled over your thighs,
the lapping rivulets at your knees, the way
your gold-brown hair was parted. At our water hole
between parkway and woods, your clothes
dropped off

and you dove into the cold spring water all of us
knew to be sacred: a dark pool released
from the dictates of nature   where we could breathe
without constraint   without the harsh odor of fear
or desire stinging our nostrils. You dove
and we cheered, living for the moment in the rare oxygen
of the underlife you had plunged into   feeling again
the icy water of time wash over us. And then you
broke the spell, bursting the surface as you held up
your hand, gashed open with that raw diagonal slash
that even now, five decades later,

wildly pulses—that wound written deep in your flesh
with the jagged edge of glass from a smashed
beer bottle—your ruined hand held up for us to witness
in all its bloody splendor   your wound, Paul: the sky
ripped open just when we needed it whole.

Dancing with Bob at Temple Bethel

We had no girls
but there were songs—
rock music beating our feet awake

"Bony Maroney" made our bodies shake
"The Twist" and "Shout"
drew the poisons out

Temple dances
were where we went to pray
and Bob would spin and wriggle like a saint

turned on a spit above unholy fire
and I would rescue him with kicks and splits
that calmed his fever   for a little while

We two had sensed that dancing
eased the pain that adolescence spiked
into our brains   so that we howled for love

that wouldn't arrive   Like wolves,
we prowled the darkest nights
until rock music   struck our lives again

like jags of lightning   from a summer storm
How many boys learned worship
at the dance

and lived to love and nurture
as grown men? Bob and I would dance
until our legs couldn't stand

our feet couldn't walk   our gasps wouldn't end
We danced ourselves alive   and then
we danced again.

For the Tough Guys

You were always waiting, like reality,
your chain hooked at the black belt cinched
over your belly tattooed with a heart
and *MOM*, Cupid's arrow pointing straight
at your grimy crotch. You were there with your
duck's-ass hair-do, leather squeaking as you reached
for your comb.

You were there when I walked Sharon home,
leaning on a Chevy hood, knocking your cleated
boot against the hot-purple fender. You were
there to give her the slow hungry look I
didn't dare give her. You were there
with your pegged pants, with your raised
third finger.

You were there when I worked at the supermarket,
stacking soup and pasta. You were there
with your garrison, with your rage, packed
in your muscle-shirt and wearing a James Cagney
frown. I woke in the hospital, still in my starched
smock, blood smeared on its stiff white page
in a language you spoke.

You were there again, this night, while I drank
cool wine with friends, revving your cycle
to make words drown. You were there in your Hell's
Angel costume, hate bulging against your thigh
like a pint of gin. Tough guys! lay down your boot-
legged guns. Bring me your knuckles for the vise
of my poem.

The Photographer at 11

Here he is, minus his camera,
the Brownie Hawkeye that has captured
shards and shrapnel and shell casings
of his life. Whoever has taken this photo
clearly loves him—you can see this
in the easy tilt of his body   in his arms,
so still and free of tension. His hands
have fallen open: barely singed leaves.
Everything about him seems tranquil,
the way a five o'clock June breeze is:
soft, to the point of losing focus.

You can see now that even his gaze
is fading   that the smile (so perfectly held
for nearly fifty years) has been smudged
or slightly erased. Who could have guessed
at his darkness, that soon he would tilt
earthwards   like a tree visited by lightning?
The dark foliage of memory obscures
and deceives. Surely, this child who breathes
in the cruel century he inhabits is a ghostly self
who watches   but will not speak.

2. After Darkness

A Summer Night

Dark country night,
how clearly I remember you:
grass on fire with darkness
the summer sky streaming
with meteors
and slow-burning flares
at the tips of cigarettes
gripped in my parents' hands
the cold flames of ice
in their drinks   glinting
as if from the signal fires
of distant stars

Such a warm summer night,
I wanted to breathe the darkness
to listen to the sizzling sparks
of words   that lifted
from those adult and familiar mouths
to dream as ice made a soft clinking
in each glass   I wanted to crawl
through the black flames
of the grass   to feel the earth
slowly warm beneath me
I wanted to be bathed
in that radiance

But Father said it was high time
I was sleeping   neatly tucked
into that nest of cotton blankets
It was time for me to sleep, said Mother
—wasn't it long past the hour when a child
falls silent? And so I was sent to bed
in the embered darkness   for flames
of the summer night
had entered the cottage with me
the dark beauty of the country night
had wound like a bright mist
around my life

And I called out in anger
through the dark window
to my parents who nursed
their drinks   who drew blue wisps
of smoke from their floating fingers
and spoke with the husky intonations
of oracles to their summer friends
I called out   I called out to them,
for these were the beings
who had showered me with perception
and I did not dream I was no longer
safe

But then the cottage door
banged open
and I heard the fall of her foot on the stair
and I knew a darkness I did not know
had come in with her   and I hid
under the silent blankets where I
forgot to breathe   And she swung her arm
as she scolded me
for filling the night with my voice
so that the buckle on my father's belt
                        flashed
in the too-still darkness   *flashed*

as its brassy edge caught
the bridge of my nose   *flashed* again
as it sent cold fire
down my mother's flesh
and again   as Father lifted me
from the bed   where my first screams
lingered   And then they saved me
with vinegar poured on the flaring wound
they saved me   with a torn flag
of ordinary brown paper
they saved me   with the cold torch
of their love

Blue Bicycles

Under the dogwood the bicycles are blue
and still, but blurred enough
to make them seem to move
                                        behind his pane
the child keeps watch   and what he sees
is real

*   *

The wheels on the bikes are blue—barely
in focus: blue as ice on a petrel's mouth . . .

The child dreams he is gliding in a park
—his father runs behind, steadying,
steadying, and then moves off   The bicycle
rises under him like a star

*   *

The wheels are coldly beautiful . . .
the child sees how right they are
for moving: he could float with them
under the milky sky, under trees blowing
like visible green wind
                                    could fly with them
into the earth's elegant houses, into the bronze
eye of a god
                        could move deliberately, paddling
like a turtle with webbed feet, navigating
narrow channels, sailing down the white throat
of time
            with them, he could go back—drifting—
he could retreat: back to his father's arms,
the meaty hands, back to the glimpsed penis,
the black shock of hair

*   *

COUNTRY OF MEMORY

Hazy and blue as a dream, light fills the room
where the child waits for life to come to him:
in his mind all things arrive—a train
with its million miniature cars comes toward him
brimming with oil and grain, comes booming
and clattering, engulfed in whistles and steam

He knows where the train must stop but sees
it will keep on going: he is the only station
on the map

* *

The hair on his father's chest grows
in a perfect cross: he is so vividly poised
on the tall rock it seems he is about to jump

The child is looking up at the sun: he sees his mother
seated on her bicycle—he sees she has come into the glare
of the rock, he sees she is gliding toward him,
naked and impossible to touch

* *

All things arrive and depart: the bicycle
pulls light into him—like a pyramid of quartz, he glows
with mineral change
The world is burning
like a photograph: it is going nowhere, but up

He begins to see
how the night empties light into time,
how silence opens—a blue flower—in the brain:

reason enough to make his soul climb, wheeling faster
and faster

CHARLES FISHMAN

Slowly Homeward

Thanksgiving, 1978

1
On our impossible drive through New Jersey
we twist and turn upon the tortured map,
munch slabs of cold turkey on stale hunks
of bread. It's been gray all week
and last night it rained. Today: a haze
of smoke and azure, peach glare under bitumen
and cobalt, streaks of King-Midas yellow
above a gas station flagpole.

2
Later, the sky is copper, apricot, new-
shined brass, old bronze. Stubble dulls
the glacial fields. The furrowed drabness
of wintering barnyards and blurred, grazed-
out hills quiets the hankering eye.

3
The road—the road has us. The car
idles at a light and takes the slow curve
along skull-white Main Street houses,
along duplicate prefab malls. Slowly,
the highway takes us homeward . . .

My parents and my wife share the front seat's
stark remoteness. I watch their heads:
the gray and thinning hair; the dyed hair,
carrot-bright; and the soft fur cap that hugs
the mind I trust above the ties of blood.

4
A falcon banks and soars above a magenta
meadow, at ease on the chill updraft—
the black wind, mother and medium.
How boldly he glides upon that mist
of water beneath the gray onrush.

5
We are not yet home but travel onwards,
past rain-glazed bridge and vacant toll booth
and the overpass to the next stretch
of boredom. It all goes dark, turns
to a stable sameness.

Slow, now, drift
with the backspin of hubcaps, with brake-
lights flashing, headlights awash in deepening
tidepools of traffic . . .

6
The mind would arrive, would arrive, but—
in truth—we are still driving. The rubber
is off the lefthand windshield blade.
Each swing across the glass beats a madcap tap-
dance: *We're alive! We're alive!* And yet—

7
There are no lamps on this blacktop highway.
The blades beat and beat as we reach for the key-
in-the-door. We talk and talk and the noise
seems to take us closer: the strained and querulous
voices, the rhythmic pump of some life beyond
our lives.

Miss Curtin

Marguerite Curtin, 68, was found clubbed
to death in her Ozone Park home Tuesday.—1995

She must have been sleeping
that dark evening in November
or reading in her upstairs bedroom,
drifting on a tide of words, then
swimming with the black but moon-
struck current all the way down river.

She must have been lulled by the rush
and propulsion of language, so that she
could hear nothing extraneous   nothing
below the surge and murmur of the pulsing
stream, nothing above the moan and pitch

of it. One thing is clear: she didn't hear
her murderer enter, didn't hear
when he clicked on the TV or, later, climbed
the stairs: immersed as she was in the books
she loved, she let the world float away.
Why would she wake when death entered?

*   *

I remember her in her brightness,
how she stood in the stark landscape
of the classroom, winsome and matronly,
at once. Her starched white blouse,
though buttoned to the throat,

could not conceal the rise and fall
of her breasts. We called her "Ma" Curtin,
though she was still in her early 30s.
Archetypal "schoolmarm," she forgave
our ignorance while encouraging

the tiniest sparks of wit and insight.
How we relished her sterness:
in her casual displays of anger or irony,
we read the grace notes of affection.
I recall her pale Irish face, her sharp tongue

and short temper, but also her nosebleeds
that taught us she, too, was vulnerable,
only older and more complete. Who knew—
if we kept hammering away at our lessons,
one day we might shine like her and live.

The Get

1
The coldest December night, a billion stars frozen
in the sky, and we two together for this journey unto death . . .
No, it was not the cemetery of short lives we were visiting
nor the morgue of aborted dreams. We were gliding
toward the end of our marriage—such a cold ride!

2
Where did we arrive if not at the place of execution?
Had not a priest in white robes invited us? And his assistants
in the murder—were they not attentive and obedient?
And did the ceiling not open then, so that the white sky
was revealed?

3
I saw you tremble as you neared, saw the tears well up—
your eyes were streaming. You were unsaying our wedding vows,
and I was your gifted partner. I saw that your breast had been pierced
by a small, fresh-hewn gravestone. You were beautiful again
in your broken body and you held the world in your arms.

4
You held the world, and it was the record of your wounds.
Yes, I recall it now, my darling, how the sky shut down
and the stars vanished like wraiths. Then the rabbi
pronounced us dead: we were strangers on the planet,
and the field we walked on was stones.

5
How cold it was! How unyielding the blackness!
Yet we returned to the train together, our lips shut
as if with a seal of fire, and there was a deep snow falling inside us.
Who were we now, as you leaned once again toward me,
as I held you tight?

After Darkness

1
Today, mother, you have become
most vulnerable: shaved   scrubbed
opened to the knife   and to the knowledge
of your surgeon, you are lost
in a drugged haze a field of opium poppies
can not equal

While you withdraw from your damaged
body that lies in false sunlight
under the cutter's hand,
I recall the thousand afternoons
I found you washing dishes
or folding clothes or setting our small
kitchen table for dinner: always
you'd be dancing from one needy thing
to another   always you'd be singing,
at least the melody of a song

Mother, we were so young and innocent
only the afternoon shade seemed dark
to us

2
Later, I grew away from you
and knew what it was to be lonely:
after the dream of your body,
where could I live so well?

Now, the earth in me stops spinning . . .
light bleeds from the evening sky
I think even you will darken a little now
that sunlight will dim in you

3
After you've been stitched, washed,
and slowly wakened   I will you
to be strong   to heal quickly   and to be
young   but then you whisper, *Daddy*
needs to rest   and it's clear, mother,
how tired you've grown

I try to remember you as you were
nearly sixty years ago, before I was
your son: your long brown hair brushed
with a reddish fire   slim waist
and slender legs   always one step
from dancing   The photos I have of you
darken and grow old

4
When I learn that you will live
that life flows back into each cell
each bone   and when you tell me, *My heart*
is set on dancing—

ten thousand sunsets shift from black
to rose   Words hold me again in their sweet
and fiery embrace

What the End Was Like

All I could see was my mother's broken face.
It had the dry pallor of a desiccated leaf.
I forced myself to look closer, to stare

at the pale lashes that barely clung
to the lids, at the thin lips that had lost
all color. Her brow was mottled snow, her nose

a slender drift of whiteness. The breath still lived
in my mother's mouth, and a few last words
tried to form there. I leaned nearer

to the bed where her soul was unhooking itself
from each bone where the white spark of her life
was preparing for departure. I saw her shiver then

and knew that the darkness of space had entered her.
The black ice of the universe had entered her.
The tips of my fingers burned.

Sunlight in Winter

For Naomi Adés

I will remember the stiffening of your body
how words left the dry hardness
of your mouth   and the way your gypsy spirit
abandoned its life-long home

It was as if an electric current
running from pole to pole   had faltered
as if the luminous beauty of the universe
had begun to fade

But I will recall your laughter and the flash
of lightning that was your smile   the way
your body woke to the first notes of music
your devotion to all you loved

for you gave us the gift of your spirit
that was sunlight in winter   and your life
warmed us and kept us safe:
even when we forgot the source of the fire

that guided us   even when your delight
in who we were   pushed us away
Mother, I will remember your bravest words:
When I get better, I'm going dancing.

My Father Washing Dishes

For fifty years he stood at his job
growing a small pension and varicose veins
that still ache when he walks

Yet he refuses to get a dishwasher
to save his back and legs: it was for her sake
he stood   and ours

Nothing has changed   He leans
against the sink   bends his stiff back
over the suds

She had cooked for him for almost sixty years
had been a partner of the first water: loyal
loving   a constant friend   and a gypsy

on the dance floor where his legs felt young
despite the pain   And so he stands and scrubs
each cup and plate   the frying pan   each fork

while the hot water pours from the tap like music.

My Father Greets the Day

Each morning he wakens
he praises God

Another day has dawned in him
and he is grateful

He is too old now to make love
but not to remember

My mother's picture waits
near his bed

and he lifts the frame to his mouth
and kisses her

His loneliness is too deep
—he cannot think the sentences—

but his lips find the glass
and his heart opens

Each day is a miracle
that begins in the region of sorrow

yet the sun finds him: he will live this day
fully

stunned each moment that she
is not with him.

My Father, Singing

January 1, 2001

Last midnight of the age
and my ageless father sings:
How wonderful you are!

The song is ancient,
but he delivers it with conviction.
Though the hour is primed for grief,

this is no time for tears. If
she had lived, they would have sung
this song together,

would have rung out the old and danced
the new world in: a duet so right
this first night of the infant century

would have blazed to gold.
My father sings, as if death might vanish
with a song. He knows his voice

no longer charms with darkened fire,
with that smooth and booming baritone
that stole her heart,

but still he sings *How wonderful you are!*
and we, his inarticulate children, are warmed
in the midst of coldness.

My Father's Heart

My father's heart stopped being angry
and started to love. It decided to love,
as if to love were a thing given to us
to decide. It decided to love, so he
put away his hate. He put away
his stern masculine face. It decided
to love, so his harsh childhood was
put away: no longer would those long-
ago days haunt him. He put more things
away: the slights and cuts and humiliations
and all his disappointments as a man.
And he put his pain away. He put these things
away and turned his heart to love. He became
a loving man, and his love outgrew his strength.

On the Jib VI

Fire Island Inlet – with my father

Gull on the guide-post at dockside
and the flayed carcass
of a fluke

on a spike behind an inch-thick rope
Tide's coming in—will the fish
choose our hooks?

Churn of engines   the mates busy
with bait: eye-pierced spearing
back-lit

with thin strips of squid   Water pumps
from the stern   engines thrum
under the scuffed deck

arched bridge in the distance
Captree Island sails away
Before a 5-ounce sinker

smacks the mucky bottom, cold beers
chill a dozen fists   Now the waves
come: the wakes

from party boats   trawlers   lobster skiffs
skiddoos   tip the coolers
and bait buckets

toward night-green water where a red buoy
dips right   then left   and chartreuse
channel markers bob

in the sea-drift near a pier's broken pilings
Skim under a two-lane bridge
laid like a freight trestle

from island to island   Hand over cash
          for the trip   cash for the pool:
                    you're looking good

today   Scud by a sand bar thick with brown-
          backed gulls   black-headed terns
                    Chug by a narrow sweep

of beach where SUV armies glitter—hubcaps
          to sun-roofs—near the washed-out jetties
                    of Sore Thumb

On prime salt marsh, sea castles rise up
          but, further out, the haze-blurred land
                    is rimmed

by weathered houses from the 30s and 40s
          when flounder and fluke were numerous
                    as sand grains

Another wake: the scarred deck dips toward
          the heaving Atlantic   Pass another Corona,
                    amigo, *por favor.*

A Space Burial

The late Timothy Leary, whose dying request was for 'one last far-out trip,' got his wish yesterday when his remains . . . were blasted into orbit. . . .—1997

This may be just what he needed—end
without closure—but mother, father, allow me

to bury you in the earth   as our people have done
for nearly six thousand years   Isn't it enough

that my mourning for you, mother, is like a pulse
that beats in me each second   that I grieve

my loss-to-be, father, even as your precious life
continues? Leave for me the night's starry blackness

the moon in its last diminishing race through late
autumnal sky   I will honor your memories, dear ones,

when you are safely at rest in the earth: together again
as you were in life   You need not pass overhead

every ninety minutes   encased in a silver satellite
Those who love you   will recall your journey

until their own lives end.

3. At the Edge

A Road in the Mountains

For my daughters

I was walking up a road
where shallow streams pulsed

Small fierce waterfalls cut through choking leaves

In the fields glimpsed through winter's trees,
not a house   not a gathered shock of wheat

Not a bird lit on a branch   nothing living cried out
I was sailing a dark river spangled by floating stars

I saw myself walking and knew the streams that surged by me
were the earth's perishing billions

Generations hurried past—sparks extinguished in an ocean—
but I was free: in you, I would continue.

East of the Hudson

After a theme by Ibaragi Noriko

These are the days that glisten like diamonds
when your pulse quickens but your heart

stays quiet: each second of your life,
something is smoldering

In the field that rises outside your window
a few small flakes flicker—pale white sparkles

that drift skyward before they are extinguished
or shear sideways

against the dark grain of the season
The wind races southeast by east

scattering the dust before it: a glimmering stream
of invisible photons

This light has the brightness of dream—bending stalks
of dead winter grass that shimmer with each breeze

This is what you love: this filled emptiness
in which each tassel and branch crackles into flame.

At the Edge

1
A warm October: goldenrod lights
the dunes, the sky a prism
of lightnings.

2
Fishing fleet on the horizon—
gray necklace of fat metal beads—
but what they trawl for, that rich ore
of ocean, is almost gone:
the striped bass my father cast for,
diminished, the sea harvested,
robbed of its blood.

3
Wind lifts the waves,
a soft lace rustle.
Beautiful things tumble
out of those sleeves:
battered twists of drift-
wood, bottle glass
ground to green or purple
splendor, this trailing hem
of the sea, an instrument
a thousand miles long: clatter
of cracked clam shells, mutterings
of smoothed stones.

4
What are we here for
if not to know beauty,
to taste the last sweetness
of being, to find the last
scatter of bones?

A Father and Two Sons

What is a father, and what is love?
Maybe it is the going out of the self
that certain men can do
when they put their children first
when they attend to the needs
of the little ones—the soul fed
with experience—as when this father
sails a striped beach towel
over his tiny son's head
over that two-year-old nakedness
closing them in to a holy space
only they can share:
under this floating pavilion,
a safe universe is born.

Or perhaps it is the same father
with his elder son, a 5- or 6-year-old,
at the blurred edge of the Atlantic.
Courage must be taught—
and caution: a backward flop
into the foam-tipped waves
a dive through the shallow chop,
no safety net but the unspoken:
I am here and I will not let you drown.
This father stands on his hands
in the sea brine, unlikely gift of fearlessness
and balance, and both sons hear what the sea
whispers: *I will not let you swim into your life*
without direction.

Jake, Sleeping

Near the Connetquot – July 1999

We took him down to the river
because he loves to see everything
and for him everything is seen
for the first time   but the rocking rhythm
of the stroller as we guided it over ruts
lulled him to sleep   and dips in terrain

the shifting alignment of wheels
pulled him deeper into his own
small darkness   The river rushed
to greet him under a brushed blue sky:
it slapped at the embankment   as if
it delighted in splashes   as if spilling itself

onto the earth might prove the first rule
of existence: *all life must change*
Then the wind came up: I could feel
Jake's dreams taking on sails:
his tiny vehicle fitted out with wings,
he would tack forever in this churning

current   Later, we rolled inland
toward the brooding realm of cedars
centuries-old oaks   flayed-bark sycamores:
we steered him clear of the broken tangle
while light squeezed down into tunnels
of palely glimmering leaves   Jake

was sound asleep when we turned back
with the stroller   and didn't see the geese
stalled in the parched grasses   or the swallow-
tails lingering, amid rudbeckia and zinnias,
and he did not wake when the 4 o'clock freight
drew its harsh music across the horizon.

First Laugh

She cradles her child, this Navajo mother,
and you can tell he is loved. His peacefulness
runs deep—you can see the tendrils of it
as they wind around his bones. *Listen.*
The sound of his sleeping is like the whispering
of the sea under a soft moon in summer.
She cradles her child and keeps him safe—
see how her arms, her hands, embrace him.
This is a rest that augurs beautiful growing,
the way a seed's slumber in the earth
prophesies the tree.

For she will blanket him with prayers and kisses,
with hummed melodies and the music
of her voice. And she will be the midday sun
to him. Come, let us wait for his first laugh.

Jake, Dancing

Jake is not waiting
for the world to end:
he is dancing   he is
running between
imaginary bases   he
catches the ball
and runs off with it
From the deck
of the pool, he leaps
again and again
Pick him up   spin him
around   lift him over
your head   where
all the darkness
of the planet swims
Throw him the ball
lift him again: this
is the moment   the
only one   Jake is
not waiting for the sky
to fall   or for night
to descend: he's
feeling the vibes
and dancing.

Early September Morning

After days of rain,
I walk in the first strong sun

to where seed heads of grass
shine silver-white

on this quiet late-summer
morning   and cows

and a young calf graze
their heads dipped in brightness

What is the sun for
if not to light the moment

when the mockingbird flies
silently   from the top rung

of barbed wire that rings
the pasture   like a wing

of unheard notes   escaping
from a guitar?

Passing September

Great South Bay, Fall 2002

All that glitters is the bay
in hazed-over afternoon sun.
The tide's in, Fire Island a thin
lifting of dark earth and sand
that crests and wavers
on this fourth day of autumn.

Fractured crab claws sprawl
on the old pier's scoured planks,
the shell of the living animal
cracked open: a husk in two unequal
halves, picked clean by the gull
that stood near, content and silent.

In this space, at the slashed edge
of the continent, a late summer day
swims back against relentless drift:
seeds, small insects, rays of light,
swept through blue September sky.

They soared and glimmered
like worlds burning out,
their diminutive lights laser bursts,
at first, but swiftly softening.

And I saw that that day, too, would fade
toward night, that all sun-lit things
would darken and contract: that beauty,
and life itself, must vanish, though tightly,
tightly, grasped.

Nocturne with and without Stars

The grass is wet. Enter the darkness.
If you can walk, do so quietly. Go
like a slow breeze or like a tree's shadow:
be in this place the way a wildflower opens
under the dews of heaven. Flow like the breeze,
so that your knees bend to that rhythm
so that your body sways to the night's softest drum.

Go farther into darkness, to where apple trees whisper
behind you and the sky opens above you its garden
of lost stars. Where are you now
but where no light can find you
and the old gods come?

Condor

He soars two miles up
on white-trimmed ten-foot
wings, the unclipped tips
curved upwards,
this last free creature of the air:
this god—seeker and devourer—
unfettered for ten million years.

The Chumash holy man knows
the condor will rise to heaven,
a thunderclap leaping
from earth to cloud, from cloud
to star. Crown prince of carrion,
he soars.

This shadow climbs the sky:
death's elder brother. Earth
is the cage   he will tear open.

At Winter Solstice

Everything is still today: filmed
with a pale blue grayness
The birches that glowed white
in late autumn sunlight have been
extinguished   *This is the cusp*
of change

Midnight will open the brightest
blossom of moon   but only if the gray veil
lifts   only if we remain awake   Now
is the time to bring in the ancient tree—
quick, while its green fires cast
such a sober light

Hold back from adornment:
it will grow darker yet before this night swells
and turns toward bleak cold morning
before desire stirs each slumbering root
and the first bright sparks of color appear
Go deeper still into waiting:

be like the mist and shadow   and praise
the oncoming night that races
toward its final wingbeat of darkness.

A Single Living Thing

A single living thing took root
in darkness
under a ledge of granite

on a scarp of glacial mountain
hidden from the light
of clouds

It grew unnoticed for decades
then centuries
until it raised a crown of branches

toward the stars
until its thick roots cleaved
to a stone embankment

and moon-sheathed boulders
were enmeshed
in what it was

Nothing but life clung to it
for a thousand years
and then, in a single night,

it fell
The shockwave shuttered
the moon

And then it was rotted timber
and loamy tunnels
for termites

a feeding ground for finches
Lichen leeched to it
and fungi extruded

their ears
Year after year, it simmered
in the sun of summer

fall breezes cooled it
winter rain iced down—
spangling each moldering twig—

and spring was the music
of its dwindling toward
nothingness

Until, in the humus and duff
that was left of it, a single living thing
took root

Opening

Celery branchlings
curl around the rotted core
of last fall's strongest plants

Mint seedlings unfurl
under roots of garlic
whitened and stiffened

by winter: they rise
at the edges
of the herb bed

Strawberry leaflets flare
in the early dusk of March
New carrot tops expose

what leaf-mulch and snow
have hidden: the beginnings
of abundance

Wild onion, as always,
flourishes: nearly impossible
to lift intact from the cold soil

Chives send up green electric probes
Tiger lilies start the long voyage
skyward

Roots, in unrestrained billions,
push downward   Half-frozen tips
of peach branches open:

each small green leaf a flame
Like mute and rooted finches,
croci brave wind and rain

and spring's first cardinal beams
to the far reaches of the planet
the red voice of his feathers.

Late Spring Quickens

After a month of rain,
I ride my bike to the beach
and give myself to the wind

blowing in from the Atlantic.
It's late in the day, too cool
to sit and read. Swings

in the make-shift playground
hang empty yet drift to right
and left, as if ghost children

sit in them, waiting for a push,
for that first swift launch
out of *ordinariness*

into the ocean of new life.

I walk the tidal sift at the edge
of this sunless bay, listening
for the quick trilled notes

of the blackbird's song
the whispered epic of the reeds
the deft music the buffeting wind makes

It's good to be silent and alone
where fate's hammer may not strike.
Someone else walked this way today

and saw the luminous spill of the waves
the combed hair of the rocks   moss-green
in late spring sunlight   tide-wrack

of smashed lobster pots on the eroded beach.

Here is the sill of the world
where each cold shimmer comforts
and rebukes.

A Field in Virginia

A wide gate swings open . . .
The hip-high grass children hid in
only two days ago has been mown.

Wade through the gold-leafed waves,
the rose-headed clover; walk
the shadowy edge of the field.

Over this river of cut grass
the sparrow hawk circles. The sun
blurs your footsteps in this world.

Walk out again when the sun
burns down the sky and the blue
sharpness of daylight is a white haze

on the hills. That fragrance you breathe
is the heart of the seed split open.
Press firmly on this green earth,

this sea of life you tread on.
Something will spring alive in you
and root down.

Wyoming Autumn

Part One

1
A black flare of cloud drags snow
out of the west, then sun returns

A cool breeze caresses your body
but with no edge, no absence of mercy,
and the day heats up, sending a hand
of pure green fire down your back
blue fire, too, fingers gold-tipped, cerulean

* *

The creek runs narrow, translucent,
and quiet over its bed of stones
The big cottonwoods and box elders
don't know the year will end: they linger
in this season, in which almost nothing
has died

* *

These fields have been here since before
the Beginning: the bent-down leaves
of the tasseled grasses are more ancient
than the showy Bighorns and each tree, distinct
in the earth and eternally beautiful, is the first
to have grown on this planet

2
I saw a large deer, a white-tail, down by the river
—he seemed to be dreaming his way across Wyoming

3
A few leaves trickle out of the cottonwoods and a fly
buzzes into my hair   Gnats swim the air: they know
this ocean of beauty

The hills that frame Johnson and Sheridan counties
are wind-scoured stone, pyramidal and barren,
though brushed at times with pear-green tones or rose,
and the rolling pasture lands below them open
into oases   into stands of mountain ash and aspen
the sunlight deems holy, so that it embraces them,
stroking each sculpted leaf to gold or ochre flame

4
Today golden leaves fall: so many break
from their arching branches, it seems a migration of pale
yellow birds—so many, the river is amazed to carry them
and the current is unable to speed them all away

* *

The high cheat-grass is bleached to a soft beige,
nearly white in the afternoon's harsh light, and the short,
thick-bladed, grasses seem lit from beneath, or within:
a toned-down apricot, lime, and scarlet

When roads lead up a mountain, they carry you into the sky

* *

I saw a brown grasshopper that flew like a large moth
and another, smaller, being that sailed with the reddest wings

I knew to linger would be to miss the sound
the bell of the afternoon makes in these hills,
and so I climbed higher, until there was nowhere else

5
Today, the grass is a sea of cottonwood leaves
The black dragon cloud that crossed the sun yesterday afternoon
brought the cold nearer   my blood felt the chill
and, this morning, the augur of colder days—colder and darker—
nibbled at my fingers

* *

Afternoon: the chill lingers, but dandelions bloom
The river runs clear again and blue fire has been brushed back
into the sky   In the sparse shadow of the hills, black Angus bulls
moan and bellow   a tortured music that seems right for the season

In the pasture at the foot of the hills, they mull the news
from the stars

* *

As soon as the sun breaks free of the clouds, a hunter
starts shooting—I walk away from the flat pop of rifle shots
and miss the ring-neck that flies up near my boots   He flies swiftly
into the field, in a jagged startled arc   and I'm left with the gift
of five feathers, black-striped on a field of tan and sienna

6
What a bleak morning! The clouds are a milky gray
the black bulls bellow   and the angular crests of the hills
seem etched into the slate of the sky   Without the blessing
of sun, the last gold leaves wear a pallor   brush darkens
and it is the already desiccated—reeds at the irrigation ditch,
the tall splayed grasses—that appear vivid and beautiful

7
I thought the harsh cry was a crow's or a magpie's
but the warning notes were a doe's   She and her companion
had seen me moving through the tangled brush . . .

I was near the stream, dreaming away the afternoon,
and she was on the verge of the wood   She was safe
from me, but her blood told her to run, and so she cried again,
in that harsh and startled voice   then bounded

into the stump-littered undergrowth of the forest

* *

A friend spoke with the clearest words—*I tremble for it!*
That is what we had felt all month: that this land,
this northern blaze of Wyoming, was one of the last chapters
in the sacred book of the earth   one of the last places
where our songs could still be heard, where they would not be
written for show or profit   but would be the true coinage
of our spirits

Here we could not remain separate from the planet
but would see that we are the earth and stars awakening,
that we are the caretakers who have come home

Part Two

1
I rise in darkness   a light wet snow is falling
The sky is grey-white and a scrim of frost
crusts the fields

The ridged bark of cottonwoods is wet and dark
on the extended branches but dry underneath
where the thinned canopy of leaves still protects it

The fields are deep in haze and a slantwise snow
skims the planet

The spare lines of trees   trunks fallen from the height
of the vanished sun   the million tufts of dry August
and September flowers   and the softly rippling waves
of the dying grass—all seems brushed with the dust of bones

2
No one has walked down to the water
and, except for the chance prints of raccoon and deer
veering off the embankment, the snow is untouched
the crust of whiteness unbroken

This late in the afternoon, the sun burns low
in the western sky: it shines white-gold light
that is blinding

* *

How the river rushes now, and how clear it runs!
It does not mind the cold that gnaws at your fingers:
it doubts the future will freeze it

Now is all rip and churn   all glint and shimmer
Nothing can stop this joy

3
This autumn's turned to winter   Not a hawk flies
through the crystallized air   the waves of fall-burnished grass
that—days ago—glowed with rainbow light   are small
white peaks   a deep range of ice-capped mountains,
miniaturized

Everything keeps still but time   and a white silence
holds the West   Only the rising sun of late October
can wake this landscape out of its uneasy sleep

4
In back of the hills, rifle shots knock   they knock insistently
against the white-streaked sky   and they travel with me
as I walk

* *

In a snowy field, dark shapes: a herd of mule deer, grazing
There are 18 of them and each lifts a graceful neck to watch
as I pass, a perpendicular shadow that slowly crosses their space

As I near, the deer get jittery and a few start to step and prance:
this is an old dance to them

* *

And now the rifle shots knock against the sky   they knock
and knock   and the report is clearly over us: death
has awakened late on this cold fall morning

And now the deer begin to leap over a fence that cuts
the grassy field   Another fence awaits them if they run too far
but, for now, escape is all they seek—and so, with utter grace,
they leap

5
This morning, hundreds of sheep in the field . . .
They shift in the breeze and swirl in circles
then, again, grow still

Last night, the gates around this pasture were locked
but the ice has escaped   the grass is soft and green
again   only the tallest peaks show white

*   *

Somewhere out of sight, someone is herding cows
The cows are not mooing: theirs is a heavier complaint
That fierce sound churns like a tide under this autumn
and it will not dissipate like a cloud

What is that loud keening? why so nearly a moan?
They are shipping cattle today   separating calves
from cows   and the stubborn cows will not stop grieving

*   *

Near the river, the bulls stand like carved black rocks
their large heads in the oat-colored grass   a few ram
their foreheads—hard as black stone—while barely moving

*   *

Late afternoon. A blaze of light streams through the clouds
then brushes them smooth   Underneath, the palest orange light:
one lake of radiance after another   The peaks of the Bighorns
are dark but the sky above them: unspeakably beautiful

6
Last night, the fathoms-deep sheep flock crossed in darkness
I remember how the flare from my flashlight held them,
how they waited for me to pass

Part Three

The sun rises again, and it is warm
The ice-capped Bighorns are blue-white in the distance
and the fields are wheat-golden in the soft shine
of the morning

* *

The sheep have migrated again: the path I walk on
is spattered with dark green droppings   but the pasture
that, just yesterday, they whitened with their bodies,
is jarringly empty

* *

A lone fly lands on my arm, drawn to the heat
and the aura of a living thing   drawn, too, to the stench
and perfume of the earth I've walked on   He is all buzz
and attention: an insomniac of the season who can't sleep
for the splendor of smells that are visited on him

* *

Except for the single fly   a sudden echo
from the plain-of-the-grieving-cows   and one quick scatter
of rifle shots firecrackering somewhere east,
silence has returned

Stillness has returned: this morning, not a deer pauses
in the shade of the trees and, in the burnished fields,
bulls do not bellow

* *

The river runs nearly silent now, and a last patch of snow
clings to the embankment's deepest cleft   For a moment,
there is no wind, and the slight breeze that pulses in the branches
of the cottonwoods barely rustles the last dry leathery leaves

* *

In the Bighorns, a long black silky shadow crosses—flash
of white wing patches   Then there is only sun   sky   the sweep
of grassy land   the black sea of white-capped mountains
the light dying out   and the cold dream of the oncoming wind

4. In Unknown Tongues

Andros Night

Darkness came up, so we walked
into town. An old woman had shown us
the shortcut: through the wood that opened
below the village, along the small turbulence
of the creek—just keep to the path and we'd be safe.
The night settled around us, but we found the road,
and the lights on the coast awoke.

Later, we met other travelers, ate with them
and drank. Simple food, good wine, and talk of home—
what could be sweeter? Someone—perhaps you, my friend—
bought another round. A bouzouki played in the distance
and the shore of the island swayed. Sweet fellowship
of the night breeze and the bottle! I think we sang
the anthem of lost brothers.

Then we headed back toward the village and the lights
of the town blew out. We walked slowly upwards,
talked of poetry and love. The stars circled above us.
But the secret path, this night, would remain a secret,
its entrance hidden in the Andros dark. What great poets
we would be, if we could drift between the worlds: poet-
angels, whose words would have the brightness of comets.

But, this night, we were merely lost: the empty
white churches and their cobalt cupolas did not waken,
nor did the roadside shrines glisten as we stepped
through starlight, bound to this earthly plane.
Here is where we would labor over our lines and here
we'd caress all we loved. We were lost in Andros night.
We circled upwards. The breeze of an old darkness chilled us.

The Light at Ligourio

In the arbor at Ligourio, grapes grow round with sun
and a family I love clusters: my friend, Dimitrios,
my dark-eyed student once; his mother, earthy
and true as Ligourio wine; his father, temperate
in the face of bureaucrats and weather. Grandfather,
too, and Great-Aunt, sit in the shade of the musky grapes.

Life has ripened them to silence, or nearly so.
They are like fruit growing sweet and still in the sunlight.
Time drifts more slowly, olive trees steep in the dusty heat
of July. Dimitrios sweetens, too, you can see this,
though he is rooted now in the burning hills of Athens.

At Ligourio, life is not a dream: his family thrives
beneath the grapes that grow round and fragrant.
They ripen with the grapes that cluster above them:
you can see how they breathe here, where quiet shadows
sweep the hand-hewn stones and white armfuls of stars gather,
as on a trellised vine that winds through the arboreal galaxies:

as on a vine that stems from the source of darkness   and delight.

CHARLES FISHMAN

Sleeping near Water

Kefallinia, 1995

1
A kid on a motorbike shows us the way.
The *pensione* is a backstreet dive:
from the bedroom, the view is rooftops,
a wedge of turquoise water, a scatter
of warped boards, open tar pots, tubs
of unwashed gravel. This is where we are,

but soon we are leaving. It is already late
in the day—the agent has gone swimming.
A raging fight with the boy brings "Uncle" back
from the beach. We would have lifted him
from the sand so we could find a sweeter place,
would have carried him back, dripping and hissing.

2
The corner room he shows us opens on water
and we fall back on the bed, at peace. The room
has a small balcony: from here, the full sweep
of the shore can be seen, the pale aqua sea
blown rose and carmine as the melting sun recedes,
then petalled into folds of purple and black silk.

Before the sun falls out of the sky and the scythe
of the lit coast darkens entirely, we drink the retsina
wine our friends gave us at parting, we eat the Ligourio
bread and cheese, we toast each other: to our health,
to love, and to the wealth of friends.

3
Water and light and the soft night breeze
blowing white curtains toward the blackened sea,
the ancient Greek sea whispering beneath us . . .
this was nearly two years ago, beloved,
but now memory surges back:

sleeping near water, on that scimitar coast
under stars, the surf breaking ceaselessly under us
where we slept, where the white curtains floated
in the soft beauty of night.

The Sea at Poros

We could have lived that way forever:
you, at ease in the sun, the sea stretched out before us.

Rocks glowed like lamps under transparent water,
as if souls might be housed there,

but there was no way down, only the mist-draped dawn
the sea like a tilted hourglass

and the sun at cloudless noon scalding each grain of sand.

Turner on his deathbed whispered, *The sun is God!*
and it is true our only star nests in his firmament,

yet as much could be claimed for the sea—
for the sea at Poros—where time ceases

in each intake of breath and a flash of fire-lit water
seems eternal.

I remember you as you were: a creature in love
with the moment, at rest in that sun-licked place

where the sea was a dream only the gods might enter.

CHARLES FISHMAN

Swans in the Mist

Markree Castle, May 2000

Mist rises on the river: even the swans
are lost in silence   This water
has forgotten its sheen   its tide pools

and current   but it holds the light
cast down from burnt edges
of charred clouds

Trees have already darkened:
the merest smudge
against the river's sinuous bed

Soon, the country will lose its shape,
all depth engulfed by a muffled blackness

This is the land that offers no escape
where the mind sails out alone
in the last flush of brightness

This is where rain is speech
where the notes of song your lips remember
are droplets of fire and poetry

Ireland, your blood fills this dark
and misty river that winds back on itself
like the curved necks of swans.

Evening on the Amalfi Coast

From this terrace over the Tyrrhenian Sea,
where four fishing boats float at anchor,
I see a dory being rowed by two standing figures.

They come closer, in what appears to be harmonious
calibration, each oar stroke timed perfectly
against the approaching night. Somewhere nearby,

another current rises: the surging strains of a symphony,
almost tidal in its flight, and then abruptly stopped.
Yes, there it is again—distant but actual—

and here on this side of the violently gold river
the sun has hurled upon the sea, two beings
in their small rocking boat pay out line

and haul it back in. They stand apart from the world,
citizens of neither this nation nor that but of the planet
—no, of the universe itself.

A Guide at the Synagogue of Rome

Her black hair catches the light
sifting in from the Tiber.
When she speaks, it is with the knowledge
of history   but from within that history.

She worships in the women's balcony:
nearer heaven   if further from the ark.
It is not what she tells us, alone, that moves
and alters us: we have long known the details.

The tapestry is not faded where she points,
for her voice burnishes each strand   and her hand,
resting on the open page of memory, stitches us together,
thread by aching thread.

A Night in Jerusalem

All night the wind was howling
Sand the color of Jerusalem
sailed with the storm and grew darker
until it took on the hue of ripened wheat
the granular texture of unrefined flour

All night it flew: a swirling heat
that scoured the Negev and encrusted
the Judean hills with the silt of dream
and memory   The wind's quick tongue
licked each brick and left it gold

then coated each pane and tile
with seething dust   At last, the sun
went dark under yellow drifts
and you slept deeply and long
The world you knew had been

vanquished   and a gold flag flapped
a crescent of hammered gold scythed
through the air: the scimitar wind
had entered you and borne you far:
this was Arabia and you were wrapped

in a chador of gold   Your tongue
was still in your mouth   but it had forgotten
how to form syllables   and your eyes
were lowered   weighed down by an old
misery   your braceleted wrists

were too pale for one who lives with the sun
and your bejewelled fingers were empty,
for you held nothing but your place
and your tenuous beauty   The hot wind
the *Hamsin*   had lifted and changed you.

CHARLES FISHMAN

Trains at Night

1
They are the journey.

Feel them. The air vanishes
before them as they near.
In their wake, the crypts of Egypt
sink more deeply into the sand,
the narcotized earth wakens.

2
Unlock the doors.
Go out into the night,
down to where the cut path
meets the road. The hum
of the living tracks will pull you further.

Let your feet hold the thrust
of the steel. The rails thrum:
this is the instrument
that will play you.

3
The train comes,
it is next to you,
and you fall into its power.
You know your short life
is unknown to it—and your small fire.

It is so close to you, you veer
with its wheels and wince
as the boxcars jolt. The shadow
of your death settles over you.

There is nowhere else.

With Jack in Egypt

Suddenly, I'm feeling old
even ancient. Sitting
in Jack's house, I listen
for the tapping of his fingers
on the 1937 Underwood
as he pops another benny
and breaks into song   into
that jazz cantata he beat
from the drum of memory
from the pulse and passions
of friends   from the dream
of connection.

It's certain that the gods
of writing visited Jack here
that his spirit lives here still
under the old scuffed floor
between the rusting coils
of the vintage electric stove
behind the half detached head-
board of Jack's old bed
and in the huge dynastic oak
that spreads astonishing wings
over each limb of this small
gray house.

I think of Jack tapping
so rapidly on those 46 keys
calling back   with each *bhikku*
word   his days with all the lunatic
greats of New York City   San
Francisco   Mexicali   L.A.
his backwoods North Carolina
home   his burials and dis-
interments   the cold jolting slides
along California's astral coast
the dark midnight freights
that held his soul captive

And then   in a down-
pour of icy January rain
I hear Jack tapping grace-
notes onto the scrolling
page: his white-magic
tantric spells   and blitzing
ecstasies   his prayers
for release from the dark
50s furies of America,
as if he were a spirit
who could not find
his Egypt.

And, suddenly, I remember
our South Bronx walk-up
earlier still than Jack's rise
to fame   Wheeler Avenue:
wide asphalt street
of my boyhood lined
with leafy trees   light
burning down through curling
branches   a soft blue flame
and the cool hardness
of stone steps that led
back into the building.

And then I see my father
in his wool shirt
and baggy khakis
his black hair already whitening,
his strong fingers tapping
the cigarette case
in his pocket   and my mother
leaning back in the sanctum
of her kitchen   almost at ease
in that blue plastic seat,
taking a few quick puffs
and letting memory play.

I remember the Philco radio
that moaned all day   and chanted
into the evening   its green
and amber dials glowing
how the black-crowned heron sky
rose with a mystic fire that threw

bright sparks of history
into each room   and how,
after bedtime, the closet door
loomed   like an unextinguished hearth
like the sealed gate of a king's crypt
in Egypt.

I remember how the night
carried me   beyond the city
lights   into a desert garden
where I walked slowly—
a prince in flowing robes—
or sat, cross-legged,
in the cotton shroud
of a prophet   and, once,
how I was set down
so gently   amid ten thousand
splendors   wearing the heavy
mask of a young pharaoh

doomed   like Jack   to die
to lie down   golden   but far
too early   in the Blue Nile sleep
of eternity. And now, at last,
I recall how I woke to the sounds
of a new epoch   to the rich
perfumes of life   to a wild sunlit
music   to ghost feluccas sailing:
with Jack in Egypt   our fingers
grasping for the last loose sheaves
of papyrus floating past   and pulling
pure pearl light   from the moon.

Wheeler Avenue

In 1948, I didn't know we had all been sliced
into races. Wheeler was my block, 1145
the two-story walk-up where my family lived.
I didn't know it was the Soundview section
of the Bronx or that the Bronx wasn't Brookline.
There was no yellow crime-scene tape, only yellow
and white chalk marks on the gray sidewalk.

1145 kicked like a nightstick when Amadou died
a few potsy-steps from Bruckner: on a clear winter
midnight, memory couldn't help him survive.
I want to speak of his crime: how he stood in that red-
brick doorway and couldn't find his tongue, how he knew
no words would help him, that nothing he could say
in the blinding light of four drawn guns would sound like

I am a man, and this is where I belong.

Dogon Figure: The Prisoner

How clearly we see him now in shadow,
in harsh light, his face darkened his elongated body
hovering in this small space. *Such a veil of beauty is on him.*

His heavy lips are kept from speech by his maker,
but each part of his being speaks: charred face torn shoulder
stump of his missing leg and the mute penis like a partially excised
tongue. For him, the centuries have sculpted a dark and fractured
crown.

The light that gilds him the shadow that devours—what do they say,
if not that his strength is still with him, that his embalmment
in blood-spattered wood his anointment with bone dust and millet
have not restrained him, that his painful amputations
have not survived his power.

Though he yearns toward us, out of the blind Sahara,
out of the Niger's ancestral heart, it is we who are held: we
who ache with desire.

A Dialogue of Brothers

Brother, what do you gain from living alone—
and what do you keep?

Vision of a split branch ripped from an oak
by lightning   night descending

like a burning mountain   daylight pouring
in torrents from the east   loneliness

deeper than a lake that never freezes
memories that race into the brush

from every path I've taken   the need
to be found again   and lost

And what of you, brother—what will you
keep?

Memory of a woman who drew me
to her breast   then pushed me away

her belief in me that warmed my coldest
nights

love of a child that gnaws at my heart
property that has owned me   that soon

will set me free   a grave with an address
a path strewn with fallen leaves

After a Long Absence,

I visit my friend. The wound
of his wife's death is closing—
he wills it to close—yet
he needs the gash to remain open,
if only the width of a paper cut.

He needs to heal but can't
let the pain escape him
—this being that has grown
so close, that has held him
when no one else remembered,
that takes into its rigid fingers
all reason to live.

It's been nearly a year, but
her face will not cease to wake him,
her voice will not fade to a hum.
He is condemned to live, to rise
on a November morning, his mouth
filled with the lilt of speech
from a woman's mouth.

CHARLES FISHMAN

In Unknown Tongues

84 yr old Russian immigrant man complains
of a burning tongue for 9 months.
—WWW Medical Alert

Who doesn't know this malady
that dulls the delights of food
and the moist textures of sex,
that cinders every intimacy?
Haven't we been aching to speak
since we arrived from that place near
the heart's equator, so that, even now,
in the heat of this sun-scorched moment,
our tongues catch fire?

We, too, have come to these silent shores,
immigrants from the world of language;
we, too, have given birth to the unsayable,
have greeted the light of each day
in unknown tongues, have gone down to sleep
with our closed mouths burning.

Moose-Moon, Montana

The road was unlit, except
for the dim spotlights aimed
by a few stars   This was Montana,
1962: year of coming darkness
year of promise and good news

On my way back home
I would meet you, your lost face
greeting me at the door
to a new life: our long stormy loving,
heavy weather of many decades

But that was after my return
from that night spent
on an abandoned highway
waiting for the deity to pump gas
and get our wheels turning again
on the black asphalt

That was long after the moose
knocked against the window glass
with its skull and asked to be
taken in—taking, instead,
the almost perfect darkness
of the universe in with its antlers

I had room in my heart to shelter
nature then, the quiet of a billion
acres of living forest   Sure,
it scared me when that moose
nosed open the door   when its beard
rasped my shoulder

but that was long before you knew
no one else could breathe the moon
in you   before we lay down in darkness,
baying like star-blown wolves

Another Life

In Maine once, nowhere near
familiar objects, an exhaust
leak broke the day into parts:
everything seemed wasted.

Ready to yield to detours,
we decided to get lost: maybe
the road would remember.
Smooth cruising was what we wanted,
not that rusting trestle of angers
and desires.

* *

Things fail—we know this.
But these hands once touched you
with a grace your body answered,
and we knew that pleasure intended
to stay: a lazy continuum.

Let things pass away! Our bodies
learned and continued loving,
drawn to the peace they knew
possible: your flesh and mine
tracing a memory more sturdy
than steel or iron.

Mysteries of Attraction

Sixteen years after being exposed to
disparlure, an entomologist still attracts
male gypsy moths during mating season.
—Source unknown, 1993

What dust was spilled on us
when we two met?

Our partings are never easy
nor our returns.

After four decades,
the fire still burns

and sparks fly between us
as if the flames were willed.

Like gypsy moths in moonlight,
the scent of our first evening lingers.

The night is filled with stars
and bright with a powerful sweetness.

Whatever gifts it brings, we will
draw near.

Shake down on us, dear life, more,
and still more, dust.

CHARLES FISHMAN

Natural Selection

A new type of giant sponge, previously unknown to science, is growing on thousands of shattered barrels of radioactive waste dumped into the Pacific Ocean. . . .

I wanted a new vase to frame summer's flowers
but nothing ceramic would do, nothing merely
smooth, mauve, streaked, hand-worked.
I wanted something that would cup the twilight
without spilling. Moonlight held back, sunlight
lingered in the future, and time drifted
in a drugged haze, but nothing could be found
to embrace me. It was the embrace I wanted:
to be sheathed, calmed by approaching darkness,
quieted, fixed in beauty and silence. I knew myself
empty, but your fingers on my face began to heal me,
your soft-lipped words so like the petals of flowers
I could put stems to them. I wanted a bouquet
of nouns and verbs to fill me, a garden of adjectives.
I would cling to shattered barrels, sway in the current
off the Farallon Islands, a new species: remote,
unrepentant, mysterious, blossoming.

A Terrain

And so I dreamt myself reborn,
a woman waking slowly: a four-poster
bed, lavender sprigs in a vase
and a deep voice trailing off
in the hallway. Curtains floated
at the opened window—such delicacy
and a startling whiteness of texture.
A warm breath billowed over me, hovered
at the tips of my body, and I knew
I was naked still beneath the quilt, cooling
from a spring morning's shower
of pleasurable heat. Which country
was this I had emerged to from out
the dark and silky fathoms? Was its shore
knowable? could I walk there, in a pale halo
of silence? Still in this bed, and the sun
pouring in now— Whose voice was it
that had reached into me, so early
in this life? Moment, clothed in mystery
and beauty, show me the name written
in my blood. I give this body to you:
take what you need, but tell me who I am.

Notes

Additional poems in this book are dedicated to individuals, as follows: "All American" to Darrell 'Dean' Walton, "Andros Night" to Don Schofield, "East of the Hudson" to Steve Piazza, "First Laugh" to Rose Butler and John Running, "Learning to Dance" to Marlene Broich, "The Light at Ligourio" to Dimitrios Smirlis, "A Single Living Thing" to Reva Sharon, "In the Woods" to David Broich & Paul Granger, and "Wyoming Autumn" to David Romtvedt and Margo Brown.

A Family Outing. Located in the Dix Hills of western Long Island, Pilgrim State Hospital was both an asylum for the mentally ill and a prison for the criminally insane. Created by the Legislature in 1929 and named for Dr. Charles W. Pilgrim, commissioner of mental health in the early 1900's, Pilgrim State opened on 825 acres with 100 patients. By its peak in 1954, it had become the world's largest psychiatric institution, with 13,875 patients.

First Laugh. In traditional Navajo culture, the child is viewed as the ultimate gift and a celebration is held in its honor when the baby first laughs.

The Get. A 'get' is a legal writ that nullifies the original contract entered into by a husband and wife in a traditional Jewish marriage.

With Jack in Egypt. Jack Kerouac wrote **The Dharma Bums** (1958) in 11 days, while living in a rented house at the corner of Clouser Avenue & Shady Lane, in College Park, Orlando.

Wheeler Avenue. Amadou Diallo was killed at 1153 Wheeler Avenue on February 4, 1998 by four NYPD officers dressed in civvies. 41 shots were fired, and 19 hit their mark.

About the Author

Charles Fishman directs the Distinguished Speakers Program at Farmingdale State University. He created the Visiting Writers Program at Farmingdale State in 1979 and served as director until 1997. He also co-founded the Long Island Poetry Collective (1973) and was a founding editor of *Xanadu* magazine and *Pleasure Dome Press* (1975). He was founder and coordinator of the Paumanok Poetry Award competition (1990-97) and Series Editor for the Water Mark Poets of North America Book Award (1980-83), and he has served as Poetry Editor of *Gaia, Cistercian Studies Quarterly,* and the *Journal of Genocide Studies*. Currently, he is Associate Editor of *The Drunken Boat* and Poetry Editor of *New Works Review*. In 1995, he received a fellowship in poetry from the New York Foundation for the Arts.

Fishman's books include **The Firewalkers** (1996), **Blood to Remember: American Poets on the Holocaust** (1991), and **The Death Mazurka** (1989), which was listed by the American Library Association as an "Outstanding Book of the Year" (1989). His other books include **Catlives** (1991), a translation of Sarah Kirsch's **Katzenleben**, and **Mortal Companions** (1977), a booklength collection of poetry. His 10th chapbook, **5,000 Bells,** will be published by Cross-Cultural Communications in 2004.

He lives with his wife, Ellen, near the Great South Bay, on Long Island.